Colors of God's Love

A Devotional Coloring Book with Scriptures

by Dianna Marcum

Warner Press, Inc
Warner Press and "WP" logo are trademarks of Warner Press, Inc

Colors of God's Love: A Devotional Coloring Book with Scriptures
Written and Illustrated by Dianna Marcum

Copyright ©2016 Warner Press, Inc

Unless otherwise indicated, Scripture quotations are taken from the HOLY BIBLE, KING JAMES VERSION. Public Domain.

Scripture quotations marked (ESV) are from the *ESV® Bible (The Holy Bible, English Standard Version®)*, copyright © 2001 by Crossway Bibles, a publishing ministry of Good News Publishers. Used by permission. All rights reserved.

Scripture quotations marked (MSG) are taken from *The Message*. Copyright © 1993, 1994, 1995, 1996, 2000, 2001, 2002. By Eugene H. Peterson.

Scripture quotations marked (NIV) are taken from the HOLY BIBLE, NEW INTERNATIONAL VERSION ®. NIV®. Copyright © 1973, 1978, 1984, 2011 by Biblica, Inc.®. Used by permission. All rights reserved worldwide.

Scripture quotations marked (NIrV®) are taken from the HOLY BIBLE, NEW INTERNATIONAL READER'S VERSION ®. NIrV®. Copyright © 1995, 1996, 1998 by Biblica, Inc.®. Used by permission. All rights reserved worldwide.

Scripture quotations marked (NKJV) are taken from the New King James Version®. Copyright © 1982 by Thomas Nelson. Used by permission. All rights reserved.

Scripture quotations marked (NLT) are taken from the Holy Bible. New Living Translation copyright© 1996, 2004, 2007, 2013 by Tyndale House Foundation. Used by permission of Tyndale House Publishers Inc., Carol Stream, Illinois 60188. All rights reserved.

Scripture quotations marked (NRSV) are taken from the New Revised Standard Version Bible, copyright © 1989 the Division of Christian Education of the National Council of the Churches of Christ in the United States of America. Used by permission. All rights reserved.

All rights reserved. No part of this publication may be reproduced, stored in a retrieval system, or transmitted in any form or by any means—electronic, mechanical, photocopy, recording, or any other—except for brief quotations in printed reviews, without the prior permission of the publisher.

Requests for information should be sent to:
Warner Press, Inc
1201 East Fifth Street
P.O. Box 2499
Anderson, IN 46012
www.warnerpress.org

Editor: Robin Fogle
Designer: Curtis Corzine

ISBN: 978-1-59317-877-2

Printed in USA

Greetings, Creative Friends:
(Yes, you ARE creative, because you were created by the Creator of the Universe!)

Many prayers have been prayed over the devotions in this book. I have asked God what might encourage your heart and point you toward Him. Also, being transparent and keeping it real were important to me.

These drawings were all done by hand; they are not computer generated or altered. And while I do enjoy a "slicked up" drawing, the only thing perfect on these pages is the Word of God. I hope you will enjoy the peaceful effect of coloring in my personal sketchbook. The wide range of subjects will hopefully keep you interested—they have kept me entertained during the creative process! My hope and prayer is that they will give you a smile and bring you some joy.

As you read the devotion and especially the Scripture, let God's Word sink into your spirit as you color the images. Adding the element of hymns or praise music during your devotional time may also be to your liking. The combination of coloring and Scripture invites us to be fully present in the moment, and I have found it invites me into a focused prayer time as well.

My recommendation for coloring these pages would be to use colored or watercolor pencils or crayons, as most markers will bleed through. If you are buying your first set of pencils, I would recommend watercolor pencils because you can use them as regular pencils, or you also can use water or a compatible liquid to dissolve the pigments, giving you two mediums in one. These are just suggestions, of course. There are so many ways to color in a page...pastels, watercolor crayons, and the list goes on!

On the drawings some areas are shaded with tiny dots. If you use a darker color to shade those parts, it will give your drawing a little more dimension and depth. For example, if you are using a medium shade of blue to color in a flower petal, use a darker shade of blue in the dotted areas. Using three color values will add even more depth.

I have a Facebook page, Drawing Closer, where I list the products I use on particular pages I have created. I will be sharing pages from this book there too, and adding products and more information. I would also love for you to post your work there to share with others. Even though miles may separate us, we can be connected through technology to share this creative process together!

I hope you enjoy your journey through *Colors of God's Love* and that you feel His love with each and every page.

Blessings,

Dianna Marcum

Strength

The Sovereign LORD is my strength! He makes me as surefooted as a deer, able to tread upon the heights. — Habakkuk 3:19 (NLT)

When trouble comes—and we know the Bible says we *will* have trouble—we need to remember to look to the Lord for strength.

Some of our troubles are just everyday annoyances. Though I may not know the exact story of your life, I'm sure you have had some experiences where you shook your head and either said aloud, muttered under your breath, or thought to yourself,

"Oh no, not again!"

Take children, for instance. Some seem prone to certain types of accidents:

> *Little ones spill milk on a regular basis.*
>
> *Your little leaguer waits until game day to say his uniform pants no longer fit.*
>
> *Your teenager locks her keys in the car—three days in a row.*
>
> *Or the most common one at our house...their shoes are lost again!*

But many times, our troubles are bigger, much bigger.... Loss of loved ones. Loss of employment. Loss of _____ (you fill in the blank).

One woman who needed God's strength to face adversity was Annie Johnson Flint. Orphaned at a young age, jostled to a couple who didn't want them, Annie and her sister were finally adopted by a loving couple, who unfortunately passed away before the girls were fully on their own.

In spite of hardship, Annie remained optimistic and cheerful. She intended to be a schoolteacher, but in her third year of teaching, crippling arthritis made it too difficult to walk. With a pen pushed through bent fingers and held by swollen joints, she penned greeting card sentiments and poems. For more than forty years, she suffered pain every day. Writing more than a few lines at a time was a difficult task.

Before these debilitating years, Annie received a promise from God, which many of her works were based on: *For all the promises of God in him are yea, and in him Amen* (2 Corinthians 1:20).

What God Hath Promised

God hath not promised skies always blue,
Flower strewn pathways all our lives through;
God hath not promised sun without rain,
Joy without sorrow, peace without pain.
But God hath promised strength
    for the day,
Rest for the labor, light for the way,
Grace for the trials, help from above,
Unfailing sympathy, undying love.

Annie Johnson Flint (1866-1932)

When we feel deflated and defeated, we need to stop, take a deep breath, and remember the Lord is our strength! We are not promised problem-free lives, but we are promised that He will be with us every step of the way.

Change

I the LORD do not change. Malachi 3:6 (NIV)

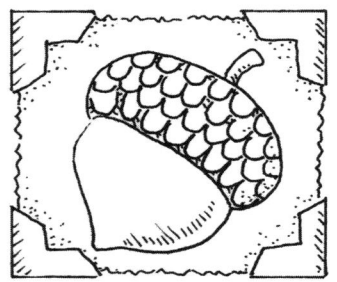

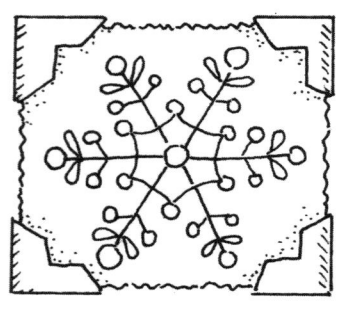

Change is a trigger word that can bring heart palpitations to the most steadfast of souls. If most of us are really honest, we do not embrace change willingly. Oh, we may enjoy a change of scenery on vacation, but nothing compares to your own bed and pillow and drinking from your favorite coffee mug after traveling for a few days. The familiar brings us comfort.

Yet, change is inevitable and comes to us all. You may be facing heart-breaking changes, like sitting on the edge of a loved one's bed, wondering how much more you or they can take. You may be separated from friends or family by death, a misunderstanding, or geographical distance, and are now experiencing extreme loneliness. Maybe sudden unemployment is causing all sorts of fears.

Even good changes, like an upcoming marriage or birth of a child, moving to a newer home, or switching to a better job—all exciting adventures—can bring anxiety and uncertainty to our lives. Even thrilling changes can leave us with an odd mixture of anticipation and fear.

Whatever changes you are presently going through, you can be encouraged with these words from our Heavenly Father Himself: *I the LORD do not change* (Malachi 3:6, NIV). Remembering to keep our eyes on Him will help us with whatever adjustments come our way in this ever-changing world we live in.

Seasons of Change

For everything there is a season,
 a time for every activity under heaven.

A time to be born and a time to die.
A time to plant and a time to harvest.
A time to kill and a time to heal.
A time to tear down and a time to build up.
A time to cry and a time to laugh.
A time to grieve and a time to dance.
A time to scatter stones and a time to gather stones.
A time to embrace and a time to turn away.
A time to search and a time to quit searching.
A time to keep and a time to throw away.
A time to tear and a time to mend.
A time to be quiet and a time to speak.
A time to love and a time to hate.
A time for war and a time for peace.

 Ecclesiastes 3:1-8 (NLT)

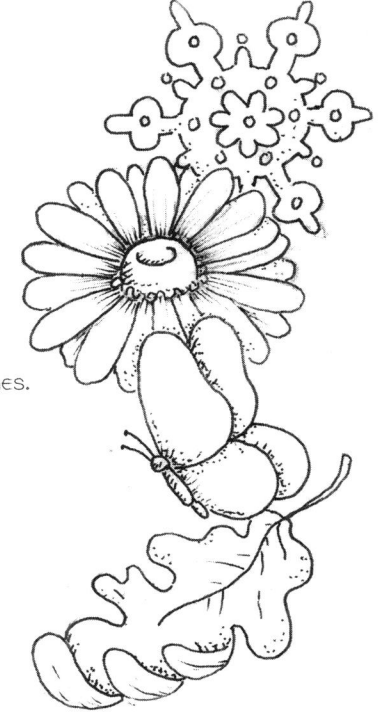

Hope

We have this hope as an anchor for the soul, firm and secure. Hebrews 6:19 (NIV)

Just as an anchor provides stability and security for a ship during a storm, hope provides the same for our souls when we find ourselves struggling in the waves of despair.

Life can be difficult. Sometimes struggles are due to the poor choices we've made ourselves or that others have made for us. Many times trials are just the result of living in a fallen world. Regardless of the circumstances, if we are giving up we are putting our hope in the wrong things.

Hopelessness is described as absolute despair with no confidence or belief that good will happen in the future. Hopelessness can result in a desire to die because people are unable to imagine any other option for their problems, and death seems the only solution. I recently attended the funeral of a 36-year-old father, son, grandson, brother, and a friend to many, who gave up hope. It broke my heart on so many levels.

There is always hope. When we feel like we have reached the breaking point, we will find the help and comfort we are desperate for if we turn our eyes to the Hope-Giver and find peace with God. God's Word encourages us, *We do not lose heart. Though outwardly we are wasting away, yet inwardly we are being renewed day by day. For our light and momentary troubles are achieving for us an eternal glory that far outweighs them all* (2 Corinthians 4:16-17, NIV). Even though we think our troubles will never end, God gives us a new perspective. Troubles *won't* last forever, and God will help us and reward us for faithfully enduring them.

Some advice for those who are seriously depressed: Do not isolate yourself. Call a friend, a relative, a doctor, or a pastor. Get yourself to a safe place where you are not alone. Suicide Prevention Hotline: 1-800-SUICIDE (784-2433)

When the whitecaps of life start tossing us around, if we keep our eyes on God, we will be able to rise above our situations, knowing that all is under His control and He will not let us sink under the waves of trials in our lives.

Additional Scriptures on Hope:

Psalm 33:22	Psalm 71:14	Jeremiah 29:11
Romans 5:1-2	Romans 15:4	1 Thessalonians 1:3
Psalm 42:5	Psalm 119:74	Lamentations 3:19-25
Romans 12:12	2 Corinthians 3:12	1 Timothy 4:10

Trust

Trust in the LORD with all your heart; do not depend on your own understanding. Seek his will in all you do, and he will show you which path to take. *Proverbs 3:5-6 (NLT)*

You may have heard someone say, "I have trust issues." When we have been hurt by someone (and seriously, who hasn't?), we may start building a wall around our heart to keep from being hurt again.

The problem comes when that wall keeps us from developing meaningful relationships. We may even try to keep God at a distance, but trusting God is essential to our relationship with Him. He is faithful and can be counted on to help us on each and every step of our journey.

When we are facing decisions and we don't know what to do, we have a reliable source for wisdom and sound advice. This short scripture from Proverbs 3:5-6 (NLT) gives us some steps to follow:

1. Trust in God not just a little, but with ALL our hearts.

2. Don't rely on our own ideas and opinions, our own human reasoning.

3. Seek His wisdom, pause, pray, and consider God's will. We shouldn't speed hastily into a solution of our own choosing, and then beg God to fix it later.

4. And lastly, God will direct our paths. Like an arrow that shoots a straight, true line, God's direction will point us in the way that is right.

This is uncomplicated advice from the Lord that will help us trust Him, not run ahead of Him, to make our own decisions. These steps are useful for complicated, important decisions and also for the smaller, not-so-important decisions. When we are of a mind to run ahead and act on our own wisdom, pausing to prayerfully reflect and consider the path the Lord would have us take will save us a lot of heartache.

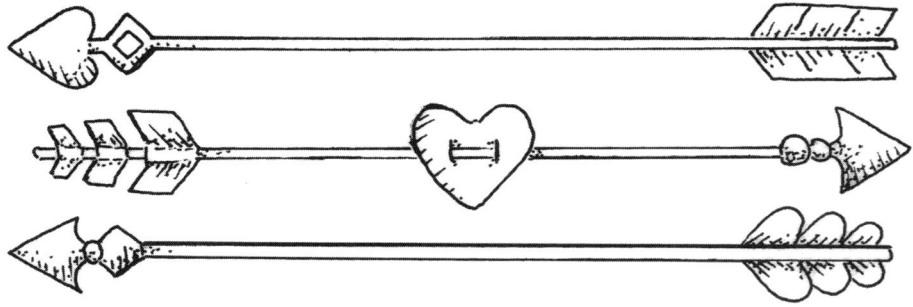

Do not conform to the pattern of this world, but be transformed by the renewing of your mind. Then you will be able to test and approve what God's will is—his good, pleasing and perfect will.

Romans 12:2 (NIV)

Focus

Turn my eyes from worthless things, and give me life through your word.   Psalm 119:37 (NLT)

Around the age of forty, I noticed my vision was a little blurry when doing artwork, so I purchased my first set of readers. They were so cute—polka dots and all—and were in the weakest strength offered. Over the years, I gradually bought stronger and stronger glasses over the counter, and for longer than I care to admit, I have been putting one pair on top of the other for close work. (Not a pretty sight!)

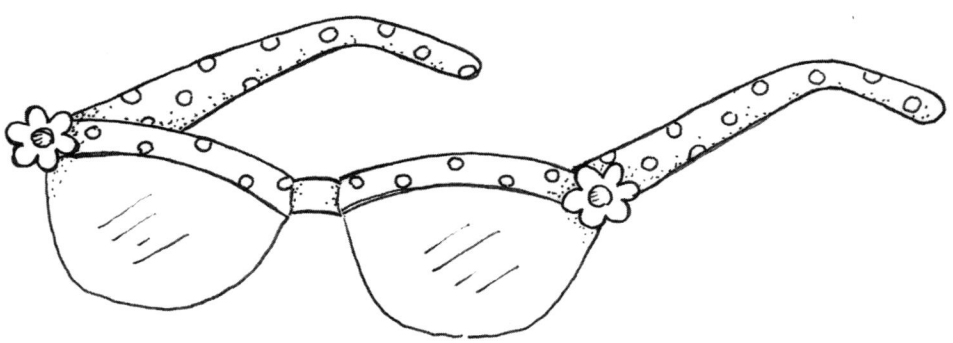

Since my long-range vision was also not as sharp as it once was, I finally went for a real eye exam. The eye doctor said, "You really don't see very well, do you?" He showed me through the "giant viewfinder" how I am seeing naturally, how I am seeing with my over-the-counter readers, and then how I will be seeing with my new trifocals—yes, from readers to trifocals in one giant leap. The difference was astounding!

I believe that is exactly how it is with God's Word. The Bible gives us spiritual eyesight. His truths bring all things into focus. The things obstructing our vision and making life blurry for us cannot be corrected with trifocals, but with turning our eyes toward Jesus.

So many distractions in life get in our way. We have a daily choice. We can choose things of little value that give us a selfish, near-sighted focus on ourselves or a far-sighted focus that keeps us too busy with events and people. We can become so distracted that we have little time to pray, read the Bible, and grow in our spiritual lives. We develop spiritual astigmatism that reflects the struggle we experience between the extremes in our lives.

Jesus knew that we would have many distractions, and the Bible gives us reminders of how we can stop, refocus, and restore our spiritual 20/20 vision.

Turn to me and be saved, all you ends of the earth; for I am God, and there is no other. Isaiah 45:22 (NIV)

I have always loved the refrain to this familiar hymn:

> Turn your eyes upon Jesus,
> Look full in His wonderful face,
> And the things of earth will grow strangely dim
> In the light of His glory and grace.
>
> — Helen H. Lemmel

When you begin to lose your spiritual focus, as we all do from time to time, turn your eyes away from the worthless things of this world. Turn your eyes upon Jesus.

Keep your eyes on Jesus. Hebrews 12:2 (MSG)

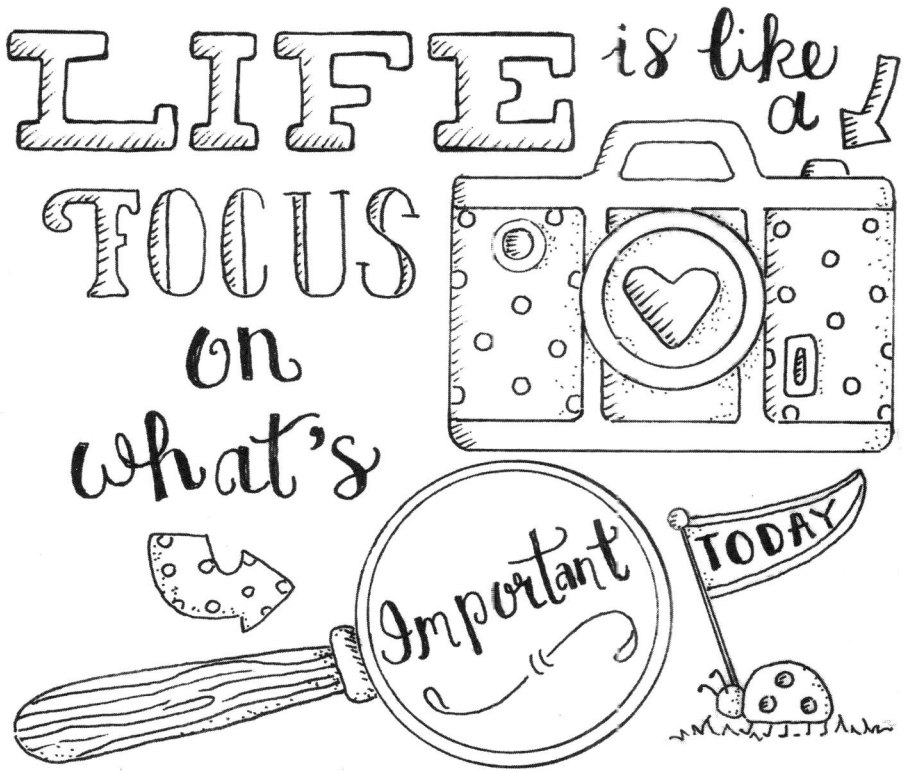

Follow

My sheep listen to my voice; I know them, and they follow me.
                                                   John 10:27 (NIV)

Years ago, I wanted sheep. We live on a farm and currently have cows, horses, donkeys, chickens, guineas, dogs, and cats. I could think of no good reason why we couldn't have sheep. My husband, who has never raised sheep, could think of several good reasons not to add them to our list of animals. The #1 reason was that he would end up taking care of them instead of me. (Truth!)

When I made another plea for sheep several years ago, he asked me why I wanted them. "I want to watch them hop and play," I told him. He assured me that he knew a lot of people who would let me come observe their sheep from time to time, and we did not need any of our own. Thus endeth the discussion. (Insert snarkey smirk here.)

With so many references to sheep in the Bible, however, my non-sheep-raising husband and I have spent some time studying their habits.

Though they are cute and cuddly when they hop and play, these are not the reasons sheep are referred to so often in Scripture. Unfortunately, sheep are not very smart animals. They graze and follow each other in large flocks. They often spread out, trying to find the best place to graze, looking for tasty grass or cool water to drink. They follow each other blindly, unaware of the dangers of the terrain or wild animals. If one sheep makes a bad choice and jumps off the cliff, the rest will follow. When they eat, they don't look around for any predators. They just keep munching and moving along, oblivious to the world around them.

Hmmm...Jesus' reference to us as sheep seems pretty accurate. We humans aren't always too smart either. We can get lost as we focus on all the shimmering and shiny things the world has to offer. Don't get me wrong—I like shimmering and shiny! But we can easily wander away from God, chasing the

things of the world, getting completely off our spiritual path, ignoring the dangers that are lurking ahead.

One of the unique things about sheep is that they recognize the voice of their caretakers. They can hear their shepherd call from a great distance and will follow the voice to safety. Not only that, even when mixed in with sheep from another herd, they will only respond to the voice they know and trust. They don't follow every voice they hear, just the one they know will keep them safe.

Jesus wants us to hear His voice and to follow His path. If we listen, we can hear His voice, even when we begin to get off the path that is best for us.

Know that the LORD is God. It is he who made us, and we are his; we are his people, the sheep of His pasture. **Psalm 100:3 (NIV)**

Lord, help us to keep our ears open to Your voice. Yell at us if You must, so we can hear You above the clamor and noise of our busy days. Whisper to us in the still of the night when darkness threatens our peace. Lead us away from the snares of this world, keep us safe, and give us Your peace. Amen.

He rescued me because he delighted in me. **Psalm 18:19 (NIV)**

God delights in you—not tolerates you, or puts up with you—

God. Delights. In. You. (Yes, you!)

Blessings

The LORD bless you and keep you. Numbers 6:24 (NKJV)

Bless you...God bless you...Bless your heart... Words we say and words we hear.

Our church once had an interim pastor who would say at the end of the worship service, "Raise your hands for the blessing." (This was quite unique in a denomination that likes to refer to themselves as the "chosen frozen"!) Then he would recite this Scripture verse over us: *The LORD bless you and keep you; The LORD make His face shine upon you, And be gracious to you; The LORD lift up His countenance upon you, And give you peace* (Numbers 6:24-26, NKJV). I remember not only lifting my hands but also my face in joyful expectancy as the words washed over me.

What does it mean to be blessed? Webster's dictionary defines it: "to hallow or consecrate by religious rite or word."

To feel the favor of being God's people, blessed by His protection, grace, mercy, and favor, should make our faces glow. Proverbs 4:18 says, *The ways of right-living people glow with light; the longer they live, the brighter they shine* (MSG). Keeping a good attitude—remembering how truly blessed we are—surely should show in our faces.

> *Keep your face to the sunshine and you cannot see the shadow.*
> — Helen Keller

Keeping your face toward the Son will give you the hope you need on shadowy days. A heavenly perspective often helps us see our struggles from a different angle.

Set your minds on things above, not on earthly things. Colossians 3:2 (NIV)

God blesses us morning and night in ways we see and in ways we overlook. In Matthew 5, Jesus offers examples of those who are blessed in His Sermon on the Mount. He tells the blessed ones, *Rejoice and be exceedingly glad* (Matthew 5:12, NKJV). The result of God's blessings is pure joy, knowing that God loves us!

Our response to being blessed by God should be praise. As Paul tells us in Ephesians 1:3 (NIrV), *Give praise to the God and Father of our Lord Jesus Christ. He has blessed us with every spiritual blessing.*

Give praise to the God and Father of our Lord Jesus Christ. He has blessed us with every spiritual blessing.

Count your blessings,
Name them one by one;
Count your many blessings,
See what God has done.
— Johnson Oatman, Jr.

Persevere

> **Consider it pure joy, my brothers and sisters, whenever you face trials of many kinds, because you know that the testing of your faith produces perseverance.**
> James 1:2-3 (NIV)

The Scripture verse for today is taken from a letter written by James, the brother of Jesus. The message was for the Jewish Christians who were weary from the persecution they were receiving because of their faith. These same words, inspired by God, encourage us when we are worn-out and drained with life's trials.

Considering hardships "pure joy" and enduring difficulties doesn't sound very appealing to most of us. Marie Curie surely must have understood this. A physicist and chemist who conducted pioneering research on radioactivity, she said these profound words: "Life is not easy for any of us. But what of that? We must have perseverance and above all confidence in ourselves. We must believe that we are gifted for something and that this thing must be attained."

God has gifted each and every one of us to do something that He has planned for us to do, but we have to dig in our heels at times to accomplish the task. The obstacles we face are part of the process, and even though often unpleasant, they help shape and mold us into vessels that God can use. Enduring difficult times is part of life, but in these times we find out what we are made of.

As we read on in the Book of James, we are assured that *God blesses those who patiently endure testing and temptation. Afterward they will receive the crown of life that God has promised to those who love him* (1:12, NLT).

Sweet Jesus,

When we face hard times, help us to persevere. And when we come out on the other side of trials, may we find ourselves stronger and more faith-filled so that we may give You the praise, glory, and honor! Amen.

The difference between perseverance and obstinacy is that one often comes from a strong will, and the other comes from a strong won't.
— Henry Ward Beecher

Wisdom

My child, eat honey, for it is good, and the honeycomb is sweet to the taste. In the same way, wisdom is sweet to your soul. If you find it, you have a bright future, and your hopes will not be cut short.
                                             Proverbs 24:13-14 (NLT)

Considered the wisest man of his time, King Solomon is accredited with the Book of Proverbs. He collected and recorded these wise sayings for future generations in Israel as a manual for living. The wisdom in Proverbs is as timely for us today as it was in King Solomon's time.

Every time we read the Bible, we can discover new truths, insights, and wisdom for our lives. When I am reading, many times something fresh will leap off the page, even when I know full well I have read that portion of Scripture many times before. At this particular time, however, the Scripture speaks to me in a different and powerful way. And that's because

God's Word is alive, just as Hebrews 4:12 says!

How many books can change with the times? I dare say none. People change, technology changes, schools of thought change, but God's Word remains. It is as relevant now as it was thousands of years ago, and it will be just as relevant thousands of years into the future.

We are all transformed by the renewing of our minds. By reading and meditating on God's Word, truth and wisdom are hidden in our hearts—wisdom that speaks to us night and day, teaching us and leading us in the right direction.

I know a woman at our church who reads a chapter of Proverbs every day, and at the end of the month, she starts over. She has done this for years, and as you might imagine, she possesses a gentle strength and wisdom.

The Bible gives us this advice: *If you need wisdom, ask our generous God, and he will give it to you. He will not rebuke you for asking. But when you ask him, be sure your faith is in God alone. Do not waver, for a person with divided loyalty is as unsettled as a wave of the sea that is blown and tossed by the wind. Such people should not expect to receive anything from the Lord. Their loyalty is divided between God and the world, and they are unstable in everything they do.* James 1:5-8 (NLT)

God has a plan for your life. The enemy has a plan for your life. Be ready and wise enough to know the difference.

Fear

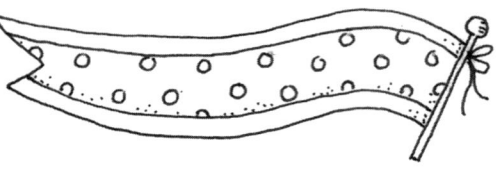

They do not fear bad news; they confidently trust the LORD to care for them. They are confident and fearless and can face their foes triumphantly.   Psalm 112:7-8 (NLT)

Are you afraid of anything? If we are honest, most of us will admit to having a few fears.

I don't like heights. In fact, my knees feel like gelatin if I am up too high and look over the edge wherever I'm standing. I also don't like to go really fast. I am just a slow and low-to-the-ground kind of gal.

My family is the complete opposite—I am surrounded by adrenaline junkies! My husband and our two daughters all like daredevil types of adventures. When our daughters were in junior high, they and my husband got on one of those giant sky dive rides. I looked up in the air as they were strapped in, waiting for the release, and prayed to God, because everything I held most dear on this earth was all tied together, way up in the air, with what looked like a giant rubber band. If you aren't fearful of heights, this probably would seem trivial to you. I was scared half to death!

I know an elementary school teacher who is terrified of clowns. I think that is so funny—I would be more terrified of a whole classroom of second graders! We each have our own set of fears that affect us, no matter whether anyone else would be afraid of those particular things or not.

As I have grown older, waiting for news, especially news that can be "bad," causes me anxiety. Whether it's waiting for test results or a family member is in crisis, whether it's financial worries or health issues, Psalm 112:7-8 reminds me not to fear bad news and to trust confidently in the Lord. Agreeing with this verse will make us:

Confident   Triumphant   Fearless

I am sure you would agree with me that feeling confident, fearless, and triumphant beats feeling anxious, uneasy, and fearful any day. Ever if the news we are waiting for is bad—perhaps even life changing—we have the Good News that God will not leave us alone, He is trustworthy, and His goodness remains constant.

These verses help me when facing fear:

The LORD is for me; I will not be afraid.   **Psalm 118:6 (NIV)**

Peace I leave with you; my peace I give you. I do not give to you as the world gives. Do not let your hearts be troubled and do not be afraid.
John 14:27 (NIV)

Remember, the Lord is coming soon. Don't worry about anything; instead, pray about everything. Tell God what you need, and thank him for all he has done.   **Philippians 4:5-6 (NLT)**

Is there something you feel God is asking you to do? Write down your fears, and then write down Scriptures to give you strength to face those fears with His help. Stop and pray, and then write down what Jesus can do through you and your fears if you allow it.

Power

I can do all things through Christ who strengthens me

Philippians 4:13 (NKJV)

Life can be hard, and we can face challenges we don't feel we are prepared for (because we aren't). I've had to do things I never thought I would do, many things I certainly never wanted to do, and several things I thought I would never be able to do, but I have done them all through the strength of Jesus.

When we have lived through a Philippians 4:13 testing, we come out on the other side a little stronger, with a bit more courage. Then, when our lives cross paths with others who are having to do the unthinkable, we can assure them that they, too, will make it through this current trial with Christ's strength, because we did.

God gives us the power to be overcomers.

The Bible reminds us that *greater is he that is in you, than he that is in the world* (1 John 4:4). God doesn't leave us to fight our battles alone. His power is available when we call upon His name because He loves us.

And may you have the power to understand, as all God's people should, how wide, how long, how high, and how deep his love is. May you experience the love of Christ, though it is too great to understand fully. Then you will be made complete with all the fullness of life and power that comes from God. Ephesians 3:18-19 (NLT)

It's not the load that breaks you down.
It's the way you carry it.

Transformation

Therefore, if anyone is in Christ, the new creation has come: The old has gone, the new is here!   2 Corinthians 5:17 (NIV)

Perhaps the proof that you a great butterfly is can go through deal of darkness something yet become beautiful

I have always been fascinated with butterflies and all the stages of transformation they go through: egg, caterpillar, chrysalis, and their final exit as a winged beauty.

Several years ago, I discovered there are professional growers/breeders of butterflies, and lo and behold, they were having their national convention that year just a few hours from where we live. I convinced our youngest daughter that it would be fun and she should go with me. Needless to say, we were in way over our heads, as the material presented was truly for professionals, not for novices like us. Besides the complexities they presented, these professionals were a tight-knit little group that knew each other well—well enough that a grown man entered the room parading and leaping in a butterfly costume (tights, wings, wiggly headpiece, and all!). When we retell the story, it still gives us fits of giggles!

Although the conference did *not* inspire me to raise butterflies (or dress like one!), the transformation this insect goes through reminds me of our own transformational journey with Jesus. Some of us are more like a woolly caterpillar than a butterfly. Some of us may be in a holding position, wrapped up in a cocoon of time alone with Jesus, while others may be just beginning to spread their wings for flight.

No matter what stage we are in, we know that Jesus keeps changing us from glory to glory, and in the end, we will emerge transformed into His likeness.

Many years ago, I told my family that I was creating a "butterfly garden." Our daughters snickered and laughed at me. Little did they know I had been researching the varieties of flowers that attract butterflies—nectar plants, as well as host plants that support a full butterfly life cycle, from laying eggs to serving as a caterpillar food source.

Planting an adequate supply of host plants gives butterflies a place to lay their eggs, which will successfully hatch and result in butterflies that will continue to visit the garden. The host plants may not be as flashy as the flowers planted for nectar, but they are part of the variety needed.

The second year after planting my butterfly garden, we literally had hundreds of butterflies in our front yard. When you walked down the front sidewalk, there was a flurry of winged insects, and it wasn't long until I heard our daughters explaining to their friends about "Mom's butterfly garden."

For our spiritual transformation we need host plants—people—too....

People like mentors who help us stay on track and hold us accountable.

Churches where we can grow and serve with others.

Godly friends to support and encourage us.

Broken

He heals the brokenhearted and bandages their wounds.
Psalm 147:3 (NLT)

Let's just face it. We are all broken people in need of a Savior. As Christians, we can all agree on this one.

But God doesn't want us to stay broken. He wants to heal our broken hearts. We can bring Him our broken pieces and ask Him to make us whole. He is able. Let those three words sink into your spirit.... He. Is. Able. Don't think for a second that He can't.

Don't believe the lie that you can't be made new through Christ's redemptive love. You have never done too much or gone so far that God won't accept you when you return to Him. Some other lies we believe are that we aren't worthy after we have failed, that no one will love us if they know the truth of our past, and that we have fallen and failed so many times that we can't be used again by God.

In truth, your story of brokenness may be just the story another struggling soul needs to hear! Maybe you will be like Isaiah, who said,

> The Spirit of the Sovereign LORD is on me,
>   because the LORD has anointed me
> to proclaim good news to the poor.
> He has sent me to bind up the brokenhearted,
>   to proclaim freedom for the captives
>   and release from darkness for the prisoners.
>   Isaiah 61:1 (NIV)

We were made to be in relationship with a variety of different people: family, spouses, friends, co-workers, people from school, clubs and organizations, church family...and often we are as quirky and colorful as a box of crayons! Relationships nurture us, shape us (sometimes they squeeze us!), and give us endless opportunities to experience and exercise spiritual maturity. Remember to be thankful for all the colorful people God has placed in your life.

A Prayer of Confidence in Dark Times

O God, early in the morning I cry to You.
Help me to pray, and to think only of You.
I cannot pray alone.
In me there is darkness,
But with You there is light.
I am lonely, but You never leave me.
I am feeble in heart, but You are always strong.
I am restless, but in You there is peace.
In me there is bitterness, but with You patience.
Your ways are beyond my understanding,
But You know the way for me.

Dietrich Bonhoeffer

Rejoice!

Always be full of joy in the Lord. I say it again—rejoice!

Philippians 4:4 (NLT)

If you haven't had the chance to read Philippians for a while, I encourage you to do so. Paul's joyful letter to the church in Philippi inspires and also challenges me. His letter doesn't dwell on his current situation (more about that later) but is filled with joy. He is encouraging others to be joyful despite whatever circumstances they are facing. In fact, Paul mentions the word "joy" or "rejoicing" 16 times!

Paul wrote the "Prison Epistles" (Ephesians, Philippians, Colossians, and Philemon) as well as 2 Timothy when he was imprisoned in Rome. Scholars disagree on which selections were written while he was under house arrest and which portions were written while he was detained in the Mamertine dungeon. But Paul's encouraging message, whichever prison it was written in, is an inspiration to us. He assures us that we do not face life's problems alone, but we do so with the Holy Spirit—through Christ in us.

After researching the Mamertine dungeon, I think it makes sense that Paul would tell Timothy to *Do your best to come to me soon.... When you come, bring the cloak that I left with Carpus at Troas, also the books, and above all the parchments* (2 Timothy 4:9-13, NRSV). The Mamertine dungeon was the most damp and dismal prison in Rome, accessed through a manhole in the street and under the marketplace. It had been a septic hole for many years and now housed the worst offenders. There the rain mixed with animal and human waste that ran off into the prison. The prisoners were chained, and the severity of their crimes determined the length of their chains. Some could sit or lie down, but many had to remain standing.

In that damp, rank place, the contaminated water often rose waist deep. The smell was horrible and toxic—no windows, no ventilation, and certainly no reason to rejoice. Many prisoners died from the nasty conditions, including rat bites and infection. Many simply lost heart and gave up. The only light prisoners would have seen was from lamps lit by the guards.

And here Paul penned words of joy, resting in the assurance that his present sufferings were temporary and that no matter what our misfortune or difficulty, God reigns supreme and sovereign. He can—and will—see us through any calamity.

Paul's time in prison certainly was a demanding and demeaning situation; however, that is not the topic he dwells on. He had learned to be content whatever the circumstances. Encouraging the people he knew and loved, Paul wrote, *I know what it is to be in need, and I know what it is to have plenty. I have learned the secret of being content in any and every situation* (Philippians 4:12, NIV).

So let's pause and ask ourselves:

How joyful are we today?

Are we overwhelmed, exhausted, worried?

We can use Paul as our example to rejoice, no matter what is going on around us.

Whatever you are standing waist deep in today—debt, depression, sickness, addictions, fear, or marital problems—whatever is weighing you down and threatening to steal your joy, remember the words of Paul. Rejoice, and be full of joy in the Lord. God knows your situation. He will deliver you and make a way for you. Until that time...rejoice!

Future

No eye has seen, no ear has heard, and no mind has imagined what God has prepared for those who love him.

1 Corinthians 2:9 (NLT)

A few years ago, I was at a conference and was awarded with a small silver pendant that was inscribed "God-Sized Dreams." Later that night when I was back in my hotel room, I was admiring the surprise gift and thinking about the words. As I pondered the sentiment, I realized I had God-sized dreams for our church, for our children, and for our grandchildren, but I had pushed aside the dreams I once had for myself.

With tears in my eyes, I prayed for God to awaken those creative, wonderful goals I once had and to give me the strength and spirit to continue to pursue them. I hadn't realized until that moment how much I missed my time in my art studio, where I have spent the larger part of my adult life. Those little words, "God-Sized Dreams," reminded me that I had some unfinished and exciting projects still ahead, and that if I would commit my time to Him, then He would make a way.

Commit to the LORD everything you do. Then he will make your plans succeed.

Proverbs 16:3 (NIRV)

I have recommitted my creative gift to God, for only He can open the doors for the dreams that He placed in my heart. He will open doors for you too.

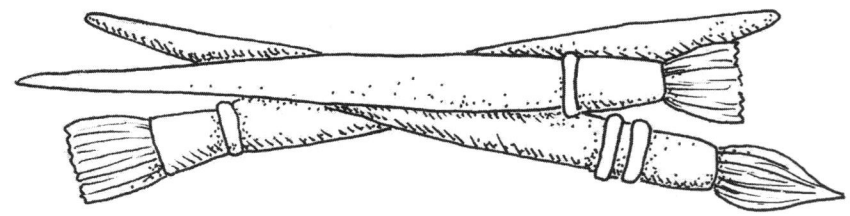

Your future is as bright as the promise of God.

Adoniram Judson

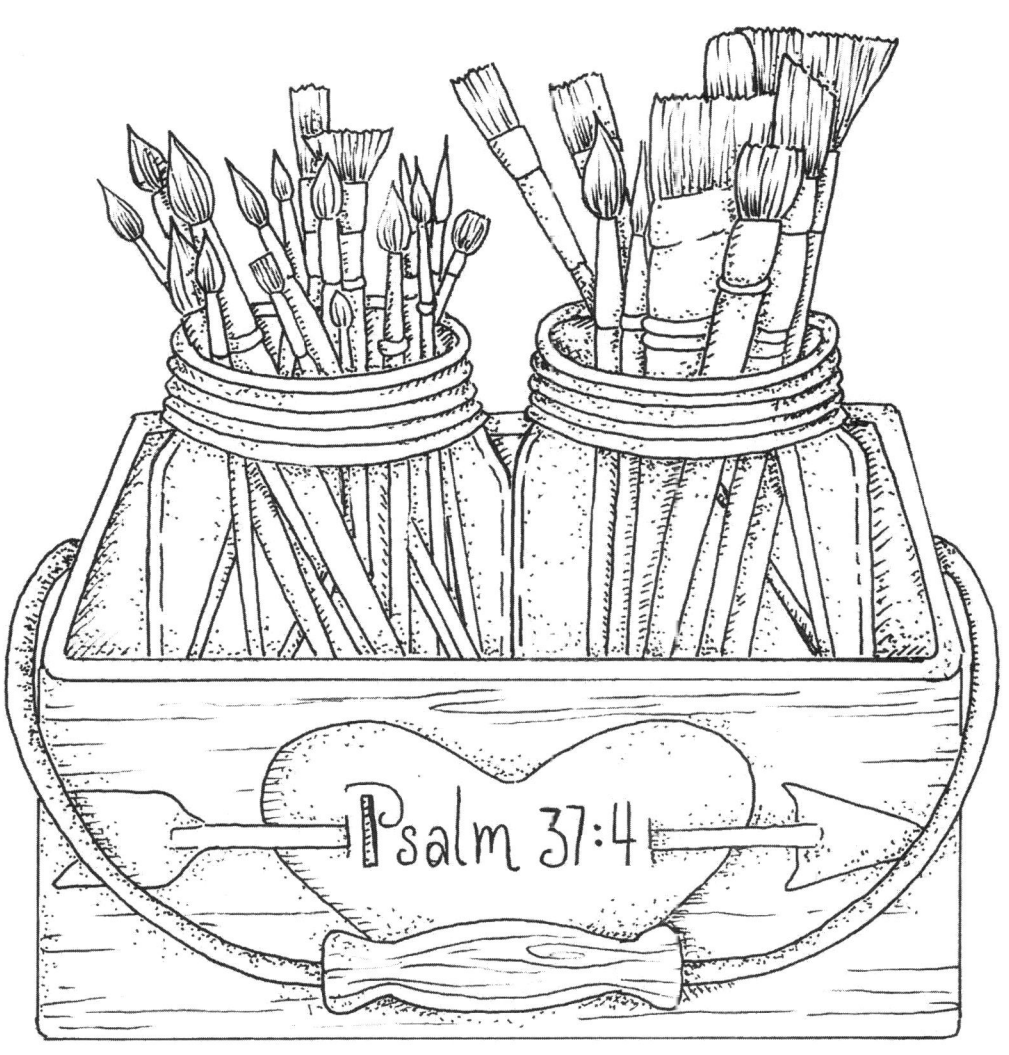

"For I know the plans I have for you," declares the LORD, "plans to prosper you and not to harm you, plans to give you hope and a future."

Jeremiah 29:11 (NIV)

Content

There is a time for everything, and a season for every activity under the heavens.
Ecclesiastes 3:1 (NIV)

In the freezing cold of winter, we wish for signs of spring—those first crocuses that pop up through the snow make us long for warmer weather. In the sweltering heat of summer, we wish for the cooler days of fall. And as the temperature begins to dip in the evenings and the days grow shorter once again, we know that winter is just around the corner. We seem to always long for something other than what we have.

We often struggle to appreciate whatever season of life we are in too. As my grandmother used to tell me, "Don't wish your life away." Savor the moments. Be content with the season of life you are in. Contentment is not the satisfaction of having everything you want—it's the awareness of how much you already have.

> *Know by the light of faith that God is present, and be content with directing all your actions toward Him.*
> — Brother Lawrence

Whatever season or transition you are in, it's temporary but it has a purpose. Don't miss what God is trying to teach you today.

> *If we are cheerful and contented,
> all nature smiles—the flowers are more fragrant,
> the birds sing more sweetly, and the sun,
> moon, and stars all appear more beautiful,
> and seem to rejoice with us.*
> — Orison Swett Marden

Godliness with contentment is great gain. For we brought nothing into the world, and we can take nothing out of it. But if we have food and clothing, we will be content with that. 1 Timothy 6:6-8 (NIV)

Learning

*Pay close attention, friend, to what your father tells you;
never forget what you learned at your mother's knee.
Wear their counsel like flowers in your hair, like rings on your fingers.*

Proverbs 1:8-9 (MSG)

Finding answers has never been easier.... Most folks don't even own a set of World Book encyclopedias anymore. When you research a topic, you don't need to go to the library and flip through index-style cards in narrow drawers. Answers to your questions can be found on Google and Yahoo with just a few clicks. Even searching for particular Bible verses and topics has been made simple through Internet sites such as biblegateway.com.

You can learn something new every day. You've probably heard that many times and even said it yourself. But it's true...*if* we keep our eyes open and pay attention.

God's Word is a wonderful resource for life-long learning. For any question we have, the Bible is always a fresh source of answers and inspiration. If we approach with an open mind and willing heart, God will gladly teach us what we need to know. Deuteronomy 4:29 (NLT) promises, *You will search again for the LORD your God. And if you search for him with all your heart and soul, you will find him.*

But, as easy as it is to draw near to God, it is just as easy to fall away. Making time daily to listen and learn is key to a growing relationship with the Lord. The words of Proverbs 19:27 (NKJV) warn us,

> *Cease listening to instruction...*
> *And you will stray from the words of knowledge.*

I plan to keep learning and studying God's Word. The more I know about Him, the more I realize how much I have yet to learn. Won't you join me?

*Anyone who stops learning is old,
whether at twenty or eighty.*

Henry Ford

Peculiar

Ye are a chosen generation, a royal priesthood, an holy nation, a peculiar people; that ye should show forth the praises of him who hath called you out of darkness into His marvelous light.

1 Peter 2:9

Peculiar...not a word that seems very positive by today's standards. A few of the synonyms are *odd, weird, strange, abnormal*, and *unusual*. But God used the word in a loving and special way, calling us to be His peculiar people seven times throughout the Old and New Testaments in the King James Version. Though other, newer translations have chosen different words to describe God's people, I've always liked this description.

The God of the universe has chosen you to be His own peculiar person in this world, to do things that only you can do.

Do what you know best:

if you're a runner, *run;*

if you're a bell, *ring.*

Ignas Bernstein

Be peculiar!
Be unique!
Be you!
God loves variety.

All kinds of things are handed out by the Spirit, and to all kinds of people! The variety is wonderful. 1 Corinthians 12:4 (MSG)
One of God's specialties is to make somebodies out of nobodies. He sees the potential in us for great things, so *let's just go ahead and be what we were made to be, without enviously or pridefully comparing ourselves with each other, or trying to be something we aren't* (**Romans 12:6**, MSG). You have the freedom to be who you were uniquely and exclusively created to be–a wonderful, one-of-a-kind child of God.

For we are God's masterpiece. He has created us anew in Christ Jesus, so we can do the good things He planned for us long ago. Ephesians 2:10 (NLT)

Patterns

Oh, that my steps might be steady, keeping to the course you set.... I thank you for speaking straight from your heart; I learn the pattern of your righteous ways.   Psalm 119:5,7 (MSG)

The patterns of our days are always changing. School, graduation, careers, marriage, babies, empty nest...our days change and our lives are rearranged, but each design for living is unique, graced with its own special beauty.

I've always enjoyed needlework, but I am not the neatest. The back of my project looks like a hot mess most of the time, but I try to make the side that shows looks as neat as I can. Life can often look like the back of my stitchery, a bunch of tangled threads that don't make sense to us. But we can be assured that God is working all things together for our good.

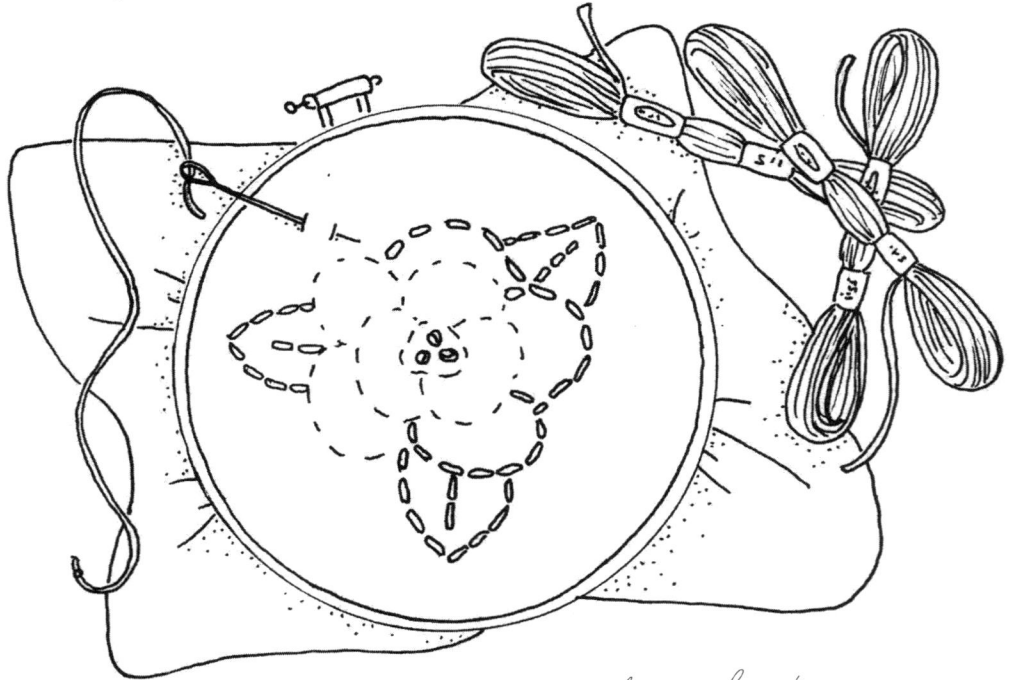

Take your needle, my child, and work at your pattern one stitch at a time taken patiently, and the pattern

it will come out a rose by and by. Life is like that;
will come out all right like embroidery.   Olive Wendell Holmes

The thief comes only to steal and kill and destroy; I have come that they may have life, and have it to the full.

John 10:10 (NIV)

Perhaps you have had some experiences that have yanked the joy right out of you. I know I have. In fact, I've had a few years that snatched so much from me I didn't know if I would ever feel like myself again.

Due to so many responsibilities, obligations, and over-commitments, I had put away the creative side of my life for a time. After being a full-time designer/artist for many (and I do mean many!) years, I knew I needed to get back in the studio, my personal "happy place." I have had to work diligently to regain my "happy" through Scripture and artwork, but I am feeling more and more like "myself" each day.

Nehemiah 8:10 (NKJV) says it so well: *The joy of the LORD is your strength.* God has designed each of us with certain talents and skills, and when we don't use them, we aren't doing what He created us to do. We were made for joy.

Solomon said, *Wisdom makes one's face shine, and the hardness of one's countenance is changed* (Ecclesiastes 8:1, NRSV). I don't think Solomon was talking about the wisdom of the world, or intelligence, but instead was taking into consideration the wisdom of keeping a good outlook on life. Keeping a positive, joyful point of view is the result of a major mind-set and change of heart.

Ada Blenkhorn was inspired to write the song "Keep on the Sunnyside" by her disabled nephew. He always asked for his wheelchair to be pushed down "the sunny side" of the street. Her words are still a great reminder for us today.

Keep on the Sunny Side

There's a dark and a troubled side of life;
There's a bright and a sunny side, too;
Though we meet with the darkness and strife,
The sunny side we also may view.

Chorus:
Keep on the sunny side, Always on the sunny side,
Keep on the sunny side of life;
It will help us every day, It will brighten all the way,
If we keep on the sunny side of life.

Though the storm in its fury breaks today,
Crushing hopes that we cherished so dear;
Storm and cloud will in time pass away,
The sun again will shine bright and clear.

Let us greet with a song of hope each day,
Though the moments be cloudy or fair;
Let us trust in our Savior alway,
Who keepeth everyone in His care.

Work

Work with a smile on your face, always keeping in mind that no matter who happens to be giving the orders, you're really serving God.

Ephesians 6:7 (MSG)

I don't know when work was given such low status in society, because working is an important part of each day. As the Book of Proverbs says, *Wise words bring many benefits, and hard work brings rewards* (Proverbs 12:14, NLT). Anyone who knows the value of hard work knows this Scripture is true. Our work can be very rewarding.

Lining up jars of homemade jelly or freshly canned vegetables always gives me a great sense of accomplishment. Shaking out the towels before folding them neatly to be placed in the closet, weeding the garden, making the bed—these everyday chores make me smile. Finishing a piece of artwork, making a deadline, the last amen at the end of a sermon—each task finished is its own reward.

Don't look upon your daily tasks as drudgery; do them the best that you can. Remember, although work may get you dirty, it is not a dirty word! A job well done will ultimately bring satisfaction and even joy! *My heart rejoiced in all my labor; And this was my reward from all my labor.* Ecclesiastes 2:10 (NKJV)

Whenever it is possible, choose some occupation which you should do even if you did not need the money.

(Adapted from a quotation by William Lyon Phelps)

Therefore, my beloved brethren, be steadfast, immovable, always abounding in the work of the Lord, knowing that your labor is not in vain in the Lord.

1 Corinthians 15:58 (NKJV)

Beginnings

In the beginning God created....   Genesis 1:1

What is my only comfort in life and death?
That I belong body and soul
to my faithful Savior Jesus Christ.

Heidelberg Catechism

The sun is beginning to come up. Soon it will peek through my linen curtains. Bible in my lap, coffee cup in my hands...the warmth of the cup matches the warmth in my heart and the love I feel. Jesus and coffee, that's how I begin my days.

Well, most of my days anyway. And on the rare occasion that I don't start with Jesus and coffee, it won't be long before the people around me know that my day didn't begin well.

I need a good beginning. I need time in God's Word, and I want coffee. Notice the difference here—I *need* Jesus desperately. I probably could just have hot water in my favorite cup and make do, but failing to spend time in God's Word is not an option.

We have a standing invitation to spend time with God. We don't have to wonder if He wants to hear from us today, or the day after, or the next...He does! *So, friends, confirm God's invitation to you, his choice of you. Don't put it off; do it now. Do this, and you'll have your life on a firm footing* (2 Peter 1:10-11, MSG).

As you begin spending time with God, you may feel His nudge to try something new. At our church we have started a "Creative Worship" monthly meeting, where we explore creative and meaningful ways to draw closer to God. Currently, I am creating a prayer journal for the ladies, with page dividers and prayers they can color and add to a small 3-ring binder. Nothing complicated, but with the hope that it will be a new beginning for some to add more depth and time in prayer.

Whatever God has laid upon your heart...just begin! If your mornings are hectic, set your alarm for 15 minutes earlier and wake before the rest of the house. In the quiet and calm, grab a cup of your favorite hot beverage and begin your day with Jesus. I promise you, it will make all the difference in your day!

Surrender

Father, if it is Your will, take this cup away from Me; nevertheless not My will, but Yours, be done.   Luke 22:42 (NKJV)

We watch a lot of old westerns—it's hereditary, I think. My father-in-law watched them for so many years that he would start laughing before the punch lines, and would often say, "Pay attention, it's gonna get good right here." Westerns follow a predictable formula—the good guys win (because they always do), the bad guys are told to "Stick 'em up," and off to jail they go with hands raised in surrender.

Surrender.... In those old cowboy movies, the bad guys didn't surrender out of trust, but out of defeat. That's not how it is for a Christian. Oh, we may not want to surrender to God at first, but it's more likely out of fear (What will be required of me?), or pride (I think I can handle this myself, thank you very much), or control issues (which are a mixture of fear and pride). In our hearts, though, we know we are loved by a Heavenly Father who can be trusted.

Surrender is the ultimate act of trust.

Jesus is our example of what it means to surrender. Because Jesus came as a man, He felt the emotions we feel. He knew what was ahead for Him and prayed to His Father that He might be spared. Yet Jesus prayed the ultimate prayer of surrender, *Not My will, but Yours, be done* (Luke 22:42, NKJV).

For many the word *surrender* brings to mind the song "I Surrender All," which was made popular at The Billy Graham Crusades in the 1940's. Judson W. Van DeVenter, the song's author, was born on a farm in Michigan, and after graduating from college became an art teacher and the supervisor of art in Pennsylvania public schools.

Van DeVenter was also an accomplished musician and an active layman in the Methodist Episcopal Church. When his friends urged him to stop teaching and go into full-time evangelistic service, he waivered for five years before surrendering to the call. Van DeVenter then traveled across the United States, England, and Scotland doing evangelistic work. In the latter part of his life, he moved to Florida and was a professor of hymnology at Florida Bible Institute. In the late 1930's Billy Graham was a student at Florida Bible Institute, and he studied and fellowshipped with Van DeVenter. Later, Graham would say that his early preaching was greatly influenced by him.

Judson W. Van DeVenter wrote more than 60 published hymns, but "I Surrender All" is by far the most well known and is still sung today.

I Surrender All

All to Jesus I surrender; All to Him I freely give;
I will ever love and trust Him, In His presence daily live.

Refrain:

I surrender all, I surrender all;
All to Thee, my blessed Savior, I surrender all

All to Jesus I surrender; Humbly at His feet I bow,
Worldly pleasures all forsaken; Take me, Jesus take me now.

All to Jesus I surrender; Make me, Savior, wholly Thine.
Let me feel the Holy Spirit, Truly know that Thou art mine.

All to Jesus I surrender; Lord, I give myself to Thee;
Fill me with Thy love and power; Let Thy blessing fall on me.

All to Jesus I surrender; Now I feel the sacred flame.
Oh, the joy of full salvation! Glory, glory, to His Name!

Enough
And he said to them, "How many loaves do you have?"
Mark 6:38 (ESV)

All four Gospels (Matthew, Mark, Luke, and John) include the miraculous story of Jesus feeding 5,000 men (and heaven only knows how many women and children) with the equivalent of a "Happy Meal." A few small loaves and some dried fish became enough to meet everyone's need. The food the disciples saw was not enough, but in the hands of Jesus—blessed, broken, and passed around—it became *more* than enough.

Too many times we focus on what we don't have instead of on what is available to us. Not that we can do the impossible in our own strength—2 Corinthians 3:5 (ESV) makes that clear: *Not that we are sufficient in ourselves to claim anything as coming from us, but our sufficiency is from God.*

If God has given you a task to do, He will also provide you with "enough" to accomplish it. When I feel overwhelmed at certain undertakings, I am reminded that in the hands of Jesus, blessed and broken, I have enough.

I Wish You Enough

I wish you enough sun to keep your attitude bright.

I wish you enough rain to appreciate the sun more.

I wish you enough happiness to keep your spirit alive.

I wish you enough pain so that the smallest joys in life appear much bigger.

I wish you enough gain to satisfy your wanting.

I wish you enough loss to appreciate all that you possess.

I wish you enough "Hello's" to get you through the final "Good-bye."

Bob Perks*

Note: The first Feeding Miracle, "*The Feeding of the 5,000*" is the only miracle (apart from the Resurrection) which is present in all four Gospels: Matthew 14:13-21, Mark 6:31-44, Luke 9:10-17 and John 6:5-15. The second miracle, "*The Feeding of the 4,000*" with seven loaves of bread and fish is reported by Matthew 15:32-39 and Mark 8:1-9, but not by Luke or John.

* Poem written by Bob Perks, www.IWishYouEnough.com. Used by Permission.

Details

And then GOD answered: "Write this. Write what you see. Write it out in big block letters so that it can be read on the run. This vision-message is a witness pointing to what's coming. It aches for the coming—it can hardly wait! And it doesn't lie. If it seems slow in coming, wait. It's on its way. It will come right on time."

Habakkuk 2:2-3 (MSG)

Write it down. Not only due to old age must I write things down, I write them down to remind myself of God's faithfulness. Journaling is not a new trend or movement, but due to technology, many "journalers" have been connected in a new way through social media, such as Facebook.

No matter how you like to record your life, you can easily find a journaling style to fit your personality. If you like to write, journals or diaries range from expensive and fancy to a spiral notebook. Some people like to keep a journal on their computer. Some even videotape themselves, talking about the special events or daily challenges of life. The method of journaling is really not as important as the process.

Journaling, for me, is a way to keep track of my life. Notes, scriptures, quotes, prayers, and precious moments are written down to keep my days from drifting together. So many times we can miss the little moments in life if we aren't paying attention, if we don't write them down. Or, we may get so busy the little things get crowded to the corners of our minds, and we simply forget. Having those moments recorded in a journal keeps them alive.

Maybe we have a big goal we haven't even given ourselves permission to think about. Write it down. Write it big. Keep it where you can see it. What many don't know is that it was God's idea to write it down (see Habakkuk 2:2-3), to keep praying, and to have faith that what we hope for will come to pass in His timing.

Either write something worth reading or do something worth writing.

Benjamin Franklin

The important thing to remember is that God has given you this one life here on earth.

Enjoy it. Record it. Remember it.

Write it BIG and remember the details!

Balance

*Great peace have those who love your law,
and nothing can make them stumble.* Psalm 119:165 (NIV)

Physical balance is not really in my skill set, and I have the ER bills and the x-rays to back that up. But the sort of balance we are all capable of is getting our priorities right.

I cringe a bit when I think about balancing priorities, remembering different seasons in my life when I was out of balance, especially in the area of working. Working, working...too many hours I have wasted away working. Sounds counterintuitive perhaps, but those with "workaholic" tendencies will understand what I mean.

When your washing machine gets out of balance, it makes a lot of noise, shimmying and shaking. My current washer even buzzes. While I am not prone to too much shimmying these days, too much of anything will eventually takes its toll.

Shop too much; you can't pay your bills. Eat too much; you can't zip your pants. Sleep too much, you can't accomplish your tasks...and the list goes on. We all know when we are getting out of balance.

The measuring stick I use to maintain my balance is very simple:

1. God
2. Family
3. Work
4. Church
5. Recreation

When I get out of whack, I find I have swapped a few numbers around and need to get them lined back up.

If we don't take care of ourselves and strive for balance, we will react to situations from a place of fear, anxiety, distraction, or anger. But when we restore balance to our lives, we are able to respond from a much healthier place.

Balance is not a one-time act, where we make the appropriate adjustments and they remain permanent. It's more like an acrobat on a high-wire who makes small adjustments while moving forward, pauses during the wild swings until stabilized, and then slowly moves forward again.

Are you satisfied that your priorities are in the correct order, or do you need to make a few adjustments? God is ready and willing to help restore the balance you need.

Create

So whether you eat or drink or whatever you do, do it all for the glory of God. — 1 Corinthians 10:31 (NIV)

We have an after-school program at our church for children ages K-6, and one thing they all love to do is create. Some may meticulously apply paint to a prayer box, while others slap all sorts of colors on theirs and carefully add sparkling jewels. Regardless of age or gender, they attack each project with enthusiasm, and they aren't trying to copy someone else. They each feel their own is the best creation of all.

I love to watch the children's creativity...before they become self-conscious of what they form and fashion with their hands. Peer pressure, also known as the "comparison game," is going to hit around junior high, and they will care more about their friends' opinions than the joy of creating. Later on down the road, creativity may be replaced with the pressure for productivity, as hobbies get shoved aside in favor of completing tasks quickly and efficiently. That's understandable. Being an adult means you can't spend all your free time pursuing hobbies, but I do think it's important to carve out some time, no matter how busy you are, to be creative.

We were created to create. In the beginning, God created... and God created us in His image. What do you like to create?

Here are a few reasons to give yourself permission to create:

1. Creating brings us joy. When God created the earth and everything in it, He paused and enjoyed what He created during each step of the process. Enjoy what you make.

2. Creating something is a way to bless others. If you make a pillow and give it to a friend, it will bless her for many years to come. Take another friend a plate of cookies, and he will think of you with each tasty bite.

3. You can decorate your own little space in the world. God could have made everything black and white and quite practical. Instead, He made giraffes and lunar moths, red-winged blackbirds and peacocks. Surround yourself with color and what makes you happy. Your creativity will bring you joy when you walk through your door each day.

4. God commanded us to use the gifts and talents He gave us. We aren't supposed to bury our talent in the ground. Whatever your hands find to do, do it with all your heart.

The list could go on, but you get the picture.... Give yourself permission to create, and then find some time to do just that. Decorate cupcakes and cookies, make a quilt, write your story, paint, color, dance. Just do it all to the glory of God!

Celebrate

They celebrate your abundant goodness and joyfully sing of your righteousness. Psalm 145:7 (NIV)

Each Sunday at our little country church, we have a time of sharing joys and concerns. We rejoice with the birth of new grandbabies, and we pray for those who have received a bad diagnosis. And if you have a birthday, we are going to sing to you! There are various reactions: a small child will revel in the attention while a teenager may blush, a pre-teen may seem annoyed, but someone who has lived a substantial amount of years will boast of their age and God's lavish goodness to have made it through another day.

I have always loved birthdays...and parties...and cake! It's important to celebrate people—God's unique gifts to this world. For one special day of the year, you are the center of attention as those who love you tell you how much you mean to them.

In Scripture we find numerous references to celebrating. Most of them are regarding the festivals of remembrance, but in Luke there is an impromptu celebration of the returning prodigal son. *Let's have a feast and celebrate* (Luke 15:23, NIV). No pre-party planning was involved, just a cause to celebrate, and the celebration was joyful. As the text goes on to say, there was music and dancing (vs. 25).

TRUE CELEBRATION COMES FROM OUR VERY SOUL AND BEING.

*It is not how much we have,
but how much we enjoy, that makes happiness.*
Charles H. Spurgeon

We need to give ourselves permission to celebrate—wear the party hat, blow the paper horn, and just let go. Plan the party or have one on the spot. Make a big deal out of special occasions, large or small. Have a shindig, bake (or buy) the cake, eat the icing, laugh, and enjoy the day. You can always count the calories and go back to ho-hum and humdrum tomorrow...they aren't going anywhere.

It is pleasing to God whenever you rejoice or laugh from the bottom of your heart.

Martin Luther

Shine

Let your light shine before others, so that they may see your good works and give glory to your Father who is in heaven.

Matthew 5:16 (ESV)

My favorite worship service of the year is on Christmas Eve. No matter what traditional texts are read or what seasonal songs are sung, the service ends with Candlelight Communion. The people of God come to the front of the church to celebrate The Lord's Supper. From the common loaf, they tear the bread to be dipped in the cup, and then from one shared candle, they light their own taper and move to the back of the room. As more and more come forward, the circle of light grows and glows throughout the sanctuary. When all have participated in taking the elements, we sing "Silent Night" with our faces aglow in the candlelight. From a dim room to one full of light...the love of Christ shines in these faces, and each year it is all I can do to stand in the wonder of it.

The light shines in the darkness, and the darkness has not overcome it.

John 1:5 (ESV)

We all know people who seem to light up the room when they walk in. As believers, we are created to shine, to radiate light like a candle in a darkened room. *The ways of right-living people glow with light; the longer they live, the brighter they shine* (Proverbs 4:18, MSG).

Too often we let the cares and worries of the world dim our lights. Jesus said, *I am the light of the world. Whoever follows me will not walk in darkness, but will have the light of life* (John 8:12, ESV). Remembering we are safe in the care of Jesus will rekindle our glow no matter what challenges come our way.

"This Little Light of Mine" is a "shine" song that many of us know the words and actions to. Although it was written as a children's song, it bacame popular with people of all ages during the Civil Rights movement of the 1950s.

This Little Light of Mine

This little light of mine, I'm gonna let it shine,
This little light of mine, I'm gonna let it shine,
This little light of mine, I'm gonna let it shine,
Let it shine, let it shine, let it shine.

Won't let Satan blow it out, I'm gonna let it shine,
Won't let Satan blow it out, I'm gonna let it shine,
Won't let Satan blow it out, I'm gonna let it shine,
Let it shine, let it shine, let it shine.

Hide it under a bushel, no! I'm gonna let it shine,
Hide it under a bushel, no! I'm gonna let it shine,
Hide it under a bushel, no! I'm gonna let it shine,
Let it shine, let it shine, let it shine.

Shine all over (insert your city here)
Shine all over (insert your city here)
Shine all over (insert your city here)
Let it shine, let it shine, let it shine.

      by Henery Dixon Loes

**A holy life will produce the deepest impression.
Lighthouses blow no horns; they only shine.**
                      D.L. Moody

The way of the righteous is like the first gleam of dawn, which shines ever brighter until the full light of day. Proverbs 4:18 (NET)

Peace

Now may the Lord of peace himself give you peace at all times and in every way. The Lord be with all of you. 2 Thessalonians 3:16 (NIV)

In Bible times, the dove and the olive branch were the peace symbols of early Christians. A flying dove with an olive branch in its beak is often found on ancient artworks.

Shalom, meaning "peace," is used as a salutation by Jewish people at meeting or parting. Shalom means much more than simply peace—it refers to a *complete* peace. This peace is a feeling of contentment, completeness, wholeness, wellbeing and harmony.

And that is what I wish for you...that as you have read the devotions and colored these pages, God has stirred your soul, your creative juices, and touched your heart somehow.

Of course, there is only one way to find TRUE shalom or peace, and that is in the Word of God and a personal relationship with Jesus Christ. Many search for fulfillment, happiness, and contentment in material possessions, money, sex, entertainment, etc. But those things do nothing to fill "that little hole in our soul" that only GOD can fill! Those things only serve to distract and prevent us from finding true peace...the shalom that can only come from the One who created and put all things into place.

Blessing of Peace

Go forth now into the world in peace;
be of good courage;
hold fast to that which is good;
render to no one evil for evil;
strengthen the fainthearted;
support the weak;
help the afflicted;
honor everyone;
love and serve the Lord.
And the blessing of God Almighty,
the God who created us,
the God who liberates us,
and the God who stays with us throughout eternity
be with you this day and forever more.

amen.

Washington National Cathedral Bulletin
Used by permission